Disasters of Leo Williams

Amber Lee Dodd

Illustrated by **Aviel Basil**

CASTLEFIELD SCHOOL
MIDDLE WAY
HIGH WYCOMBE
HP12 3LE

OXFORD
UNIVERSITY PRESS

Hello! My name is Amber and I write plays, short stories and children's books.

I once lived in a castle with a very loud owl. But now I live by the sea with a half-Bengal cat, who still firmly believes she's a wild animal.

I wrote Leo's story because I am a horrible worrier, too, and I often battle through my own Disaster Lists. I wanted to let my fellow worriers know that you're not alone, and that we all get frightening thoughts sometimes. But it's surprising how many go away when you talk about them, or when you get the courage to face your fears. Remember, being brave doesn't come without being scared first.

Amber Lee Dodd

Sometimes, I wake up in the morning and think about all the things that could go wrong.

For example: I might say the wrong thing in class. Then everyone would look at me. I would get so embarrassed that I might explode!

Or I might go to the toilet and find that it's full of wriggling snakes!

I could even be really unlucky and get hit by lightning on the way to school!

I call this my Disaster List. I think about it a lot – especially when I'm trying to go to sleep.

But there's one time when all those worries stop. When I'm playing the drums. Drumming always makes me feel better. Well, it used to, until I got a part in the school talent show …

I didn't want to be in the talent show. It happened by accident. I was just scratching my head, when Mrs Fowler said, 'Who wants to play in the rock band at the talent show?'

Mrs Fowler must have thought I was putting my hand up, so she put my name on the list.

CLASS ROCK BAND:

LEO WILLIAMS - DRUMS

ROSE WILLIAMS - SINGER

ALICE TAN - GUITAR

My sister Rose saw my name on the list. She told our parents all about it.

'Guess what?' she said. 'Leo's going to play the drums in the rock band! I'm going to be in the band too!'

My parents started making a big fuss about it. They said they were really proud of us both, and couldn't wait to see the talent show. So then I had no choice! I had to be in the show.

After that, Rose, Alice and I spent most of our lunch breaks rehearsing. We practised and practised, until we sounded really good.

But as the performance got closer, my Disaster List got bigger. I just knew I would forget how to play the drums. Or I would mess up the song. Or, worst of all, my costume would be too big. It would fall off, and everyone would gasp in horror! I knew I had to get out of performing.

So, on the morning of the talent show, I drew bright red spots all over my face with a felt-tip pen.

'I can't do the show tonight, Mum. I'm sick,' I said, adding a cough.

'Oh dear, that's a shame, Leo,' said Mum. 'But I think you'll feel a bit better later. You could come and watch Rose and Alice.'

I nodded. I wanted to hear Rose sing and Alice play. I knew they sounded great. They would be fine without me.

That afternoon, we all sat in the front row to watch the performance. Some Year 4s did a brilliant Bhangra dance. Then the Year 5 football team did tricks that made my parents cheer.

For a moment, I almost wished that I was up on stage too. Then Mrs Fowler introduced the next act.

'Our next performers are from the Year 3 rock band!' she exclaimed.

The lights dimmed and Rose and Alice came onto the stage. Alice played the first chord on her guitar, but Rose just stood there. Her mouth opened slightly, but no words came out.

My parents looked worried. The audience started murmuring. Rose looked like she was about to cry.

Thank goodness that's not happening to me, I thought. But then I felt awful. Because it shouldn't have been happening to Rose, either! She knew the song, we all did. But she had never done it without me before. Alice looked straight at me.

I knew she wanted me to help.

I took a deep breath and got to my feet.

'What are you doing, Leo?' Dad said.

There was no time to answer. I jumped onto the stage. My heart was thumping. My hands were sweaty. My Disaster List popped up in my head again. But then I closed my eyes and thought about how hard we had all practised. And how much I wanted to play. I picked up the drumsticks and tapped them together.

'One, two, three,' I yelled. Then I hit the drums.

Alice played the first chord again and then Rose began to sing. When we finished, everything went quiet. Then everyone in the hall started clapping. My parents stood up, cheering! We had done it!

We took a bow. As we did, I remembered how worried I'd been. How I had spent all my time thinking about disasters. I'd never stopped to think what would happen if everything went well. Or how I'd feel if it did.

It felt amazing.